FIVE-MINUTE

FIVE-MINUTE

PASTA SAUCES

FIVE-MINUTE

PASTA SAUCES

MICHAEL OLIVER

Crown Publishers, Inc.
New York

TO LAURA AND CATRIONA

Text and illustration © 1996 Breslich & Foss

Conceived and produced by Breslich & Foss, London.

Photography by David Armstrong
Styling by Susie Gittins
Illustrations by Madeleine David
Designed by Roger Daniels
Original design by Lisa Tai
Home economist: Michael Oliver
Editor: Janet Ravenscroft

Published by Crown Publishers, Inc.
201 East 50th Street, New York, New York 10022.
A member of Crown Publishing Group.
Random House, Inc. New York, Toronto, London, Sydney, Auckland

CROWN is a trademark of Crown Publishers Inc.

Printed in China

Library of Congress Cataloging-in-Publication Data is available upon request

ISBN 0-517-70154-5

10 9 8 7 6 5 4 3 2 1

First American Edition

CONTENTS

THE FIVE-MINUTE APPROACH

No one is quite sure when pasta was invented. According to some, the ancient Romans ate it; others believe that the traveller Marco Polo introduced it to Italy from China in the 1200s. Whatever its origins, pasta is a nutritious and exceptionally versatile food. It is rich in carbohydrates, has a low fat content and it releases energy into the body over a long period of time. There are hundreds of pasta shapes and delicious sauces with which to serve them. Most important of all in these busy times, pasta can be turned into an attractive and nourishing meal in a matter of minutes, without resorting to jars of processed sauce or the microwave oven.

One of the great things about Italian cooking is its simplicity: it does not rely on fancy techniques, scores of ingredients or cleverness for its own sake. In the same vein, the five-minute pasta sauces in this book do not involve a complicated range of ingredients or difficult cooking methods. They can be prepared (more or less) in the time that it takes to cook the pasta. They aim to combine a few contrasting or complementary textures and flavors to create tasty dishes that can be served as a main course or in smaller quantities as a first course. In cooking of this kind, the quality of the ingredients is crucial: if they are poor, there is little to disguise them. Apart from that, it is hard to go wrong.

Though the ingredients vary, most pasta sauces are based on tomatoes, oil, eggs or cream. There are examples of each kind of sauce throughout this book, with a few more offbeat ones thrown in for good measure. Each recipe suggests a range of pasta shapes to partner the sauce, and some variations or alternatives to the basic recipe. The quantities given serve four as a main course.

WHAT PASTA IS MADE OF

Flour and water pasta: Most pasta is made from a special, hard variety of wheat called durum wheat, which is ground to make a coarse, grainy flour, or semolina. The simplest pasta consists of durum wheat flour and water, mixed into a dough, shaped and dried. Most of the pasta sold in packets – such as spaghetti, macaroni, and penne – is of this type. Flour and water pasta is usually served with sauces based on tomatoes or olive oil which partner its nutty texture well.

Egg pasta: Egg pasta – pasta all'uova – has a richer, softer texture and is made from durum flour, or the softer wheat flour, and eggs. A little water or olive oil is sometimes added. Dried, packaged egg pasta is available from most food stores: it is usually made into

Pasta is a nutritious and versatile food.

noodle shapes such as tagliatelle or fettuccine, or into broad sheets like lasagne, though it is occasionally used for smaller shapes. Pasta all'uova is the ideal accompaniment to richer, cream-based sauces. Purists would argue that there is no substitute for home-made egg pasta – though the high-quality shop-bought varieties are perfectly good, and a lot more practical for the busy cook.

"Fresh" pasta, pre-packed and refrigerated, is now available from many supermarkets and delis. Unfortunately it varies greatly in quality. While, to the five-minute cook, it has the advantage of cooking more quickly than most dried pasta, its taste and texture is often disappointing. Try experimenting with different brands until you find one that suits you. If you are lucky enough to have a store near you which sells freshly made (unrefrigerated) pasta, go for that. Remember, though, that it must be used immediately.

Flour-and-water and egg pasta are the two basic types of pasta, though there are other variants such as wholemeal pasta, which contains wholemeal flour, and a range of colored pastas which take their hues from natural ingredients such as tomatoes, saffron or spinach. There is even a black pasta, which is colored with cuttlefish (squid) ink!

THE MAIN SHAPES

Though there are only two basic kinds of pasta they are made into a multitude of shapes. The differences between shapes are often subtle and can easily be missed – at a casual glance, tonnarelli and spaghetti may look the same, but in fact the former is square in section, while spaghetti is round. Just to complicate things, the same shape will often have different names in different parts of Italy. But though there are hundreds of pasta shapes, they can be broken down into a few broad groups which are described here.

Long pasta: The best-known pasta shape is probably spaghetti, but there are many other forms of long pasta strands, from thin, flat linguine and trenette to the bizarre looking fusilli lunghi bucati – which are like long hollow springs. The list below shows some of the more useful and widely-found shapes. In general long pasta shapes are best suited to lighter sauces based on olive oil, eggs or tomatoes. However, some of the chunkier varieties, such as fusilli lunghi or bucatini, a sort of fat, hollow spaghetti, will combine well with heavier sauces. Most long pasta shapes are made from flour-and-water pasta and are sold dried in packages.

Spaghetti: The classic pasta shape. Ideal with thin, tomato, egg- or oil-based sauces.

Spaghettini: The ending *-ini* means small. Spaghettini is just a thinner version of spaghetti.

Linguine: A kind of flat spaghetti, ideal with seafood sauces.

Trenette: A narrower version of linguine, almost square in section. Traditionally served with pesto.

Bucatini: A thicker, hollow version of spaghetti. The diameter of the pasta and of the hole varies. In its thickest form, it looks like long, straight elbow macaroni.

Fusilli lunghi: Spiral pasta tubes, which look like elongated springs. Suited to chunkier sauces. Fusilli lunghi bucati have a hole running through them.

Flat pasta: Flat, noodle-like pasta ribbons are usually made from pasta all'uova, and can be bought dried or "fresh" (see above). Fettuccine and tagliatelle are the most commonly found shapes. Both are thin, flat noodles, but fettuccine is usually narrower than tagliatelle.

Both are sold straight, or curled into nests. Less well-known shapes include pappardelle, tonnarelli and lasagnette. The delicate, slightly absorbent texture of these egg noodles is perfect with creamy or buttery sauces.

Tagliatelle: The classic egg noodle, perfect with rich or creamy sauces.

Fettuccine: A little narrower and thicker than tagliatelle.

Paglia e fieno: The combination of green and white fettuccine is known as paglia e fieno – "straw and hay." The green noodles take their coloring from finely-chopped spinach which is mixed into the pasta dough. Paglia e fieno is often served with a sauce of ham and peas.

Pappardelle: A broad egg noodle. Usually at least half an inch wide. Sometimes made with saw-toothed edges.

Tonnarelli: A narrow, square-section noodle.

Lasagnette: A broad flat noodle with a wavy edge.

Lasagne: Broad, flat sheets of egg pasta, used in baked dishes.

Pasta tubes: Tubular forms of pasta are usually made from flour-and-water dough and are a good accompaniment to chunkier sauces or to tomato-based sauces. Short, hollow macaroni are perhaps the best-known form of pasta tube, but other versatile varieties include quill-shaped penne. Tubes can be smooth (*lisci*) or have ridges (*rigati*).

Rigatoni: Wide short tubes, usually ridged. The widest varieties are used in baked dishes rather than with sauces.

Elbow macaroni: The most famous of the tube shapes. A short, narrow pasta tube, with a slight curve. The outer surface may be smooth or ridged.

Penne: "Quills" – short, straight tubes cut aslant at both ends. They are made with a smooth surface or with ridges.

Torchietti: A delicate "little torch" shape made from a sheet of pasta rolled into a thin cone. Unlike the other tube shapes, torchietti are usually made from egg pasta.

Amori: Sometimes called cavatappi, these are like a corkscrew-shaped macaroni.

Other shapes: Pasta makers' inventiveness knows no bounds. There are shapes resembling seashells (*maruzze, conchiglie*); snails (*lumache*); cartwheels (*ruote di carro*); radiators (*radiatori*), and even a specially-commissioned variety of pasta invented by a car designer to hold the maximum amount of sauce (*marille*)! These "special" shapes are all made from flour-and-water pasta, and are sold dried. Some of the commoner varieties are given below:

Farfalle: Literally "butterflies" – a distinctive bow-tie-shaped pasta, with crimped edges.

Conchiglie: "Conch shells", available smooth or ridged.

Fusilli: A flat spiral-shaped pasta, like the thread of a screw.

Orecchiette: "Little ears" – dimpled circles of flour and water pasta.

Then there are the classic stuffed pasta shapes, like ravioli and tortellini, made from egg pasta and filled with meat, cheese or spinach. Since they cannot be made in five minutes, they fall outside the scope of this book, which anyway focuses on five-minute *sauces*, not pasta making. However, with a simple dressing of cream or olive oil, ready made ravioli can form a quick and nourishing meal.

Some useful shapes for the cupboard: With so many varieties of pasta it would be easy to fill the pantry with nothing else. For Italians, part of the pleasure of a pasta dish is the match between the shape and texture of the pasta and the sauce accompanying it. However, since storage space is always at a premium in the kitchen, it is best to stock up on a few of the most useful and versatile shapes, and to buy more specialized ones as needed. Exploring the wide range of shapes available is part of the fun of pasta cooking.

Some key varieties for the cupboard are: spaghetti; penne or fusilli; tagliatelle or fettuccine; linguine. Most of the recipes in this book can be served with one of these key varieties of pasta, though a range of suggested pasta types is given with each sauce.

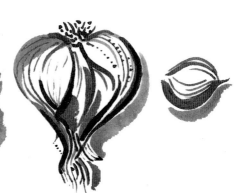

How to Cook Pasta

A confession: most pasta takes just a little longer than five minutes to cook. The exceptions are fresh pasta (see above) and special quick-cooking varieties like three-minute spaghetti (which has little grooves cut into its surface to speed the cooking process). However, the idea of this book is that you can prepare the sauces themselves in five minutes, leaving you time to check the pasta when you have finished.

The amount of pasta you will need per person depends on whether you are serving the dish as a first course or a main course. (All the recipes in this book are written to serve four people as a main course.) As a main course, you will need about 4 oz (100 g) of pasta per person; as a first course, 3 oz (75 g) of pasta is generally sufficient.

To cook pasta properly you will need a good large saucepan, ideally with a lid, so that you can quickly bring the water back to the boil once the pasta has been put in. A large pot is important because the pasta needs plenty of water to absorb the starch it will give off and so prevent it from sticking together. You should never use less than 4 quarts (2 liters) of water in total, even if you are only cooking a small amount of pasta. Bring the water to a fast boil and then add two heaped teaspoons of salt for every quart (1 liter) of water. The salt will give the pasta flavor.

When the water is boiling furiously, add the pasta all at once. Bring the water back to the boil (if your pan has a lid put it on for a few minutes to help return the water to the boil, but do not leave it on throughout the whole cooking process), give it a stir and leave the pasta to cook. Stir it a few more times during the cooking process, to make sure it is not sticking.

Cooking times: Different shapes and makes of pasta will require different cooking times. Thin strands like spaghetti or linguine will generally take about seven minutes, chunkier shapes like rigatoni or fusilli a little longer. However, exact cooking times will vary from brand to brand. Follow the time advised on the package, but start testing the pasta before the end of the recommended cooking time. Fish a piece out with a fork or draining spoon, let it cool and then bite it. It should not be hard and starchy (undercooked) or limp and bodiless (overcooked). The aim is for the pasta to be *al dente* (literally "to the tooth") – firm and offering a little resistance to the bite. If in doubt, always err on the side of undercooking, and remember that, even with the heat turned off, pasta left to sit in the pan will continue to cook until the water has cooled. If you want to stop the cooking process, drain the pasta.

Draining and dressing: As soon as the pasta is done, drain it into a colander and give it a few shakes to remove excess water. Never rinse the pasta – the coating of starch released during cooking helps the sauce cling to it. Place the drained pasta in a serving dish, or back in the pan while you combine it with the sauce. Do not let it sit undressed, otherwise it will begin to stick together (you can add a little olive oil or a few spoonfuls of the cooking water to keep it moist). Toss the pasta with the sauce thoroughly, so that it is well coated but not swamped. Pasta is not just a platform for sauce. The pleasure of a good pasta dish lies in the combination of the sauce with the taste and texture of the pasta itself.

KITCHEN EQUIPMENT

Making pasta dishes requires no complicated equipment or tools. Most of the items below will be standard in any kitchen.

Knives: Two good knives are essential: a larger one for chopping vegetables and meat; a smaller one for paring vegetables or slicing delicate ingredients. Keep knives sharp by sharpening them little but often. You will also need a large chopping board on which to work. A mezzaluna- ("half-moon") shaped blade with handles at each end is useful for chopping herbs quickly, but you can manage without one.

Kitchen scissors: A sharp pair of kitchen scissors can save the five-minute cook a lot

of time. They are useful for chopping herbs and salad leaves and for snipping ingredients like prosciutto or smoked salmon.

Pans: You will need at least one large saucepan, ideally with a lid, in which to cook your pasta (see above). A steamer, which can be fitted over the pan while the pasta is cooking, is a useful time-saver when cooking ingredients such as asparagus or spinach. Alternatively you can use a separate steamer over its own pan of water.

Most of the sauces in this book can be made in a single large frying pan, though some also call for a second pan. Non-stick pans with good heat conductivity are best.

Colander: A colander, or at a pinch a large sieve, is essential for draining cooked pasta.

Spoons and tongs: A slotted spoon is useful for fishing out pasta to test whether it is cooked. Spaghetti tongs are not really necessary – a couple of forks or a fork and spoon will do the job just as well. You will, of course, need wooden spoons for stirring pasta and making sauces.

Food processor: A few of the recipes in this book call for a food processor to make herbs or nuts into pesto-like sauces. The processor should be fitted with the rotary chopping blade. The sauces *can* be made the traditional way, using a mortar and pestle, but not in five minutes.

Parmesan grater: Parmesan cheese is the traditional and perfect accompaniment to many pasta dishes. It is should be grated fresh as needed. If you grate it too far in advance it oxidizes unpleasantly. You can grate parmesan using the finest setting on a normal cheese grater, but if you eat pasta a lot, it may be worth getting a parmesan grater. This is a small, steel mill, with a handle on top. You put a piece of parmesan inside and turn the handle to grate it. The grater can be stored in the refrigerator with a piece of parmesan inside, until needed.

The pre-grated parmesan sold in tubs or packets is *definitely not* recommended (see *Parmesan* below).

Garlic press: Self explanatory and very useful. Crushed garlic has a stronger flavor than chopped garlic.

Lemon zester: A few of the recipes call for thin strips of citrus rind. A lemon zester is the best tool for this, but the finest setting on a cheese grater is a workable alternative.

Olive pitter: An olive pitter will save time when stoning olives. Some garlic presses come with one built into the handle.

THE CUPBOARD

Most pasta sauces, and all five-minute ones, do not involve a complicated range of ingredients, but are based on a narrow range of staples such as oil, tomatoes or eggs, to which fresh ingredients like vegetables, meat or fish are added. The pleasure of the recipe comes from the combination of tastes, colors and textures, rather than from artifice or elaboration. The quality of the ingredients is therefore vital.

Keep a supply of the basic ingredients in the pantry. You can make many five-minute pasta recipes just from these staples, and can augment them with other specially bought ingredients. Try to keep the cupboard tidy and well laid out, so that you can find things quickly – the five-minute schedule does not include time spent rummaging in the back of cupboards!

Canned tomatoes: Cans of chopped Italian plum tomatoes are best, and form the base for many of the sauces in this book. Keep two or three tins on hand. Cans of chopped tomatoes with basil and garlic already added are a useful time-saver.

Crushed tomatoes: Mid-way between chopped tomatoes and tomato puree, crushed (pulped) tomatoes come in jars or cartons. They are useful in sauces which need a smooth, thick tomato base. Passata is a smoother more refined version, with the pips sieved out.

Sundried tomatoes: Sundried tomatoes have an intense rust color and a wonderfully salty flavor. The ones packed in oil (rather than sold absolutely dry) are easiest to use.

Garlic: Buy it fresh, by the bulb, and store it in a cool dark place. It will keep for about ten days (so there is no point in stockpiling lots).

Olive oil: Good quality olive oil is very important, because olive oil is the starting point for so many recipes. There are several grades ranging from "extra virgin" (the product of the first pressing of the olives – dark green and strong tasting) through "virgin" (less strong, the product of the next pressing) to "pure" (more refined, yellower, milder in flavor, and cheaper). Ideally you should have two sorts. Use a pure or virgin olive oil for general cooking purposes. Keep a bottle of extra virgin olive oil for dressing pasta dishes. It is a mistake to heat extra virgin olive oil, because it spoils the flavor.

Dried chilies: Sold in packets, dried chilies are used in spicy pasta dishes like *Pancetta and Chilies* (page 52), or in smaller amounts just to add a little zip – as in some seafood sauces. With their red husks and yellow seeds, they also contribute a dash of color.

Nutmeg: Nutmeg is used in cream- or egg-based sauces such as *Cream, Parmesan and Nutmeg* (page 20), where it offsets the richness of the cream. Buy nutmegs whole and store them in a jar, grating a little as needed.

Saffron: Saffron imparts a golden color and distinctive flavor to cream-based dishes. Supermarkets and delis sell little sachets of saffron strands or powder. Keep one of these in the cupboard. If using saffron strands, they should be crumbled and softened in a teaspoonful of water before use.

Anchovies: Anchovy fillets can form the basis for a quick seafood sauce (see page 44). Anchovies are sold dry in salt, or canned in oil. Canned ones are more convenient to use.

Capers: Capers are sold rolled in salt, or pickled in vinegar or brine. The salted variety need a thorough soaking in water to remove their saltiness. The pickled kind just need a brief rinse.

Black olives: Black olives should be glossy and full of flavor. Look out for Italian olives, and for Greek kalamata olives. It is best to buy olives loose rather than canned. Canned olives are often grey and lacking in flavor, especially the pitted ones.

Herbs: If possible, use fresh herbs rather than dried ones. This is particularly important in the case of herb and oil sauces such as *Goat's Cheese with Thyme and Pine Nuts* (page 22) where the thyme is a key ingredient and a dried herb would not have time to soften. Many supermarkets now stock fresh herbs.

Basil: Nothing goes with tomatoes quite as well as basil, and there is no real alternative to fresh basil. Store it in a cool place (not in the refrigerator, which is too cold), with the stems in a little water. Some food shops now sell whole basil plants, which can be kept on the kitchen windowsill. Basil leaves should always be torn, rather than chopped – they release more of their flavor that way. Basil is a very delicate herb, and the leaves should not be torn until just before you need to use them, because they can quickly wilt and blacken.

Parsley: Flat leaf parsley will keep for a few days if stored in a cool place with the stems in a little water. Dried parsley is not a good substitute. As with basil, some food shops now sell whole parsley plants.

Thyme, sage, oregano, rosemary: Best bought fresh, as needed, though they can be used dried in recipes where they are not a major ingredient and will have time to soften and release their flavor. For example, dried rosemary works perfectly well in *Pork Sausage and Rosemary* (page 58).

Prosciutto: Prosciutto or Parma ham is a salty air-cured ham with a translucent amber coloring. If you have difficulty in finding it, substitute another dry-cured ham. Where possible, alternatives are given in the recipes that use prosciutto.

Pancetta and bacon: Pancetta is a kind of coarse, air-cured Italian bacon, streaked with fat. It is available smoked and unsmoked (the unsmoked variety is more common). In pasta sauces it is usually used cut into cubes or thick matchsticks, and is best bought either in thick slices or a single piece. Thick-cut bacon works well as an alternative to pancetta.

Parmesan: Parmesan has become a generic name for a particular hard, grainy Italian cheese, though in fact the original parmesan, *parmigiano reggiano*, is made only in a small region of northern Italy (a real parmesan cheese has the words "Parmigiano Reggiano" printed on the rind). Made from cows' milk, parmesan has a low fat content and a characteristic granular texture. It smells nothing like the tubs of overpoweringly "cheesy" pre-grated parmesan, which you should avoid if at all possible. Buy a piece of parmesan and grate it fresh, as needed. Wrapped in wax paper, it will keep in the fridge for several weeks. *Grana padano*, which is made in the area of the Po Valley, is similar to parmesan. It does not have quite the same taste and texture, but is less expensive.

Pecorino: Pecorino is a hard sheeps'-milk cheese, with a stronger taste than parmesan. It is often used in southern Italy as an alternative to parmesan, and should be stored in the same way (see above).

1
CHEESE SAUCES

CREAM, PARMESAN AND NUTMEG

Ingredients
8 fl oz (200 ml) cream
1 oz (25 g) butter
A pinch of nutmeg
Salt and freshly-ground black
    pepper
2 oz (50 g) freshly-grated
    parmesan
Parsley, for decoration

Toss cooked, drained pasta
with sauce and serve at once
with freshly grated parmesan.
Serve with fettuccine,
tagliatelle or fusilli.

This is a classic pasta sauce, often served with
noodles as "Fettuccine All' Alfredo" – a dish named
after the chef who invented it. Like many Italian
recipes, it is very simple, using straightforward
ingredients to create something surprisingly greater
than the sum of its parts.

The nutmeg is important in this sauce – it offsets
the cream and brings out the taste of the cheese.
Take care not to burn or boil the cream when you
are reducing it in step 1. Stir it regularly and use a
medium to low heat.

With a green salad, this rich sauce makes a filling
main course or, in smaller quantities, a satisfying first
course. Cream-based sauces like this are usually
served with ribbon-shaped pasta, such as fettuccine
or tagliatelle, rather than thin shapes like spaghetti.

1 *Simmer cream and butter
in a small pan, stirring
regularly until mixture has
thickened and reduced by a
third.*

2 *Add pinch of nutmeg and
season with a little salt and
freshly-ground black pepper.*

3 *Stir in grated parmesan
and remove pan from heat.*

GOAT'S CHEESE WITH THYME AND PINE NUTS

Ingredients
4 oz (100 g) pine nuts
5 Tbs good-quality olive oil
2 Tbs fresh thyme leaves,
   finely chopped
8 oz (200 g) goat's cheese,
   broken into small pieces
Salt and freshly-ground black
   pepper

Serve with spaghetti or
spaghettini.

This is a simple sauce for a summer's day: hot, herby olive oil, the tang of slightly-melted goat's cheese and crunchy, toasted pine nuts. Alternatively, use a soft, herby cheese and good-quality olive oil. Served with spaghetti or spaghettini, this recipe will make a light main course.

Dry-roasting the pine nuts gives them a fuller, nuttier flavor. Pre-heat the pan (there is no need to add oil) and stir the pine nuts over a medium to high heat for a minute or two, taking care not to burn them.

It is best to use fresh thyme for this recipe – dried thyme does not have the same flavor and its texture is not much different from green sawdust. Strip the leaves from the stems and chop them roughly. If you do not have fresh thyme, you can substitute chopped flat leaf parsley.

1 Heat a small pan over a medium to high heat. Add the pine nuts and dry-roast until golden brown. Remove and set aside.

2 Heat the olive oil in the pan over a medium heat. Add the thyme leaves and cook for a few minutes.

3 Place the cooked, drained pasta in a serving bowl with cheese and pine nuts. Pour over hot thyme, oil and seasonings and toss well.

HERB, TOMATO AND MOZZARELLA

Ingredients

8 oz (200 g) mozzarella
    cheese
8 cherry tomatoes
2 Tbs fresh thyme, chopped
6 large basil leaves, torn in
    large pieces
Salt and freshly-ground black
    pepper
6 Tbs extra virgin olive oil

Toss cooked, drained pasta
with sauce and serve at once
with freshly-grated parmesan.
Serve with spaghetti or
spaghettini.

This sauce requires virtually no cooking. The hot
olive oil melts the cheese and takes up the flavor of
the chopped herbs. Fresh herbs are essential but you
can vary the mixture according to what is available –
oregano, chervil or flat leaf parsley are all good
substitutes, though try to include some basil, since
few herbs complement tomatoes quite as well.

You can add variety further by including drained
capers, pitted black olives or pine nuts in place of
some of the herbs. A mixture of yellow and red
cherry tomatoes will make this summery sauce even
brighter. It is important to use a good-quality olive
oil in this recipe, because it is such a central
ingredient.

Similarly, it is worth taking trouble over the
mozzarella. There are two main varieties – cow's
milk mozzarella and the more expensive *mozzarella
di buffala* which is made from buffalo's milk and has
a better flavor. If you have a choice, try the latter.

1 *Cut mozzarella into small
dice. Cut tomatoes in quarters
with a sharp knife.*

2 *Place mozzarella and
tomato pieces in a large
bowl. Add thyme, basil
leaves and a little seasoning.*

3 *Heat oil in a small pan
until it starts to sizzle. Pour it
over the ingredients in the
bowl.*

Gorgonzola Sauce

Ingredients
4 oz (100 g) gorgonzola,
    dolcelatte or other blue
    cheese
8 fl oz (200 ml) cream
1 oz (25 g) butter
Salt and freshly-ground black
    pepper

Toss cooked, drained pasta
with sauce and serve at once
with freshly-grated parmesan.
Serve with fusilli, penne, or
macaroni.

The piquant taste and soft texture of gorgonzola
make it a natural for a five-minute pasta recipe. Melt
it into cream and butter, add a little seasoning, and
you have a full-bodied pasta sauce which makes a
quick and satisfying main course. An orange and
watercress salad complements the cheese well. Serve
it with some crusty bread to mop up any leftover
sauce!

There is no need to confine yourself to gorgonzola:
dolcelatte is a good substitute, though you may want
to increase the amount you use, given its milder
flavor. Blue Stilton or Danish blue are also
tremendous.

At the seasoning stage taste the sauce before you
add any salt. Blue cheese is already quite salty, and
once you have put salt in, there is no going back.

This thick, full-flavored sauce needs to be served
with a chunky variety of pasta. Wholewheat fusilli,
with their slightly nutty texture, are particularly good.

1 *Crumble the cheese into small pieces.*

2 *Stir cream and butter in a small pan over medium to low heat until butter has melted.*

3 *Stir in cheese until melted and mixture has thickened and reduced slightly. Season to taste.*

PAUPER'S SAUCE

Ingredients
3 fresh eggs
4 oz (100 g) freshly-grated
    parmesan
2 oz (50 g) butter, cut into
    small pieces
Salt and freshly-ground black
    pepper
A pinch of ground nutmeg
    (optional)
Basil, for decoration

Serve with spaghetti, rigatoni,
penne or fusilli.

Pauper's sauce is so called because you can make it
when you have almost nothing in the pantry. This is
one of the simplest and most satisfying pasta sauces.
It is ideal for a quick family meal or as a late-night
snack and can be varied by adding chopped parsley
or basil leaves to the egg mixture before tossing the
pasta. To make a slightly richer version, use four egg
yolks instead of whole eggs in step 1, or add a little
cream. For a lighter version, replace the butter with
2 Tbs olive oil.

   The eggs should still be slightly runny when the
sauce is served – the consistency of the inside of a
good omelette. The warmth of the pasta will
generally be enough to bring them to this smooth
consistency but, if you are uncertain, you can place
the pan briefly over a very low heat to help the
process. If you do so, take care not to overheat it or
you will end up with an unpleasant combination of
pasta and scrambled eggs.

1 *Beat the eggs lightly in a
large bowl.*

2 *Add the parmesan and the
butter. Season with salt and
pepper and, if you are using
it, a pinch of nutmeg.*

3 *Stir cooked, drained pasta
into sauce, which will
become thick and smooth
from the heat of the pasta.*

RICOTTA AND SPINACH

Ingredients

1 lb (400 g) fresh leaf
  spinach (pre-cooked
  weight), washed and
  drained
4 oz (100 g) ricotta
3 oz (75 g) freshly-grated
  parmesan
2 oz (50 g) pine nuts
1 oz (25 g) butter
Salt and freshly-ground black
  pepper

Toss cooked, drained pasta
with sauce and serve at once
with freshly-grated parmesan.
Serve with tagliatelle,
pappardelle or fettuccine.

Young leaf spinach can be steamed in a few minutes over the pan in which the pasta is cooking and can be used in lots of ways to make a quick sauce. Spinach and ricotta are often used as a filling for stuffed pasta shapes like ravioli or tortellini. This recipe adds parmesan and pine nuts to make a thick, pesto-like sauce, which is nourishing and full of flavor. It is important to chop the spinach well in step 1, so that it will amalgamate with the other ingredients when cooked. If at step 3 you feel that your sauce is still too thick, you can place the spinach, ricotta, and parmesan in a food processor and process until smooth, and then warm them through. Do not place the pine nuts in the food processor – stir them in afterwards, otherwise they will be chopped too fine to add much crunch.

To vary this basic spinach and cheese combination, add a handful of raisins to create a sweet and savory sauce.

1 *Chop spinach thoroughly and steam for 2-3 minutes over pan of salted, boiling water.*

2 *Drain steamed spinach, pressing out as much water as possible with a wooden spoon.*

3 *Place spinach in a shallow pan over low heat. Stir in remaining ingredients until combined and warmed through. Season to taste.*

2
FISH AND
SEAFOOD SAUCES

TUNA WITH BLACK OLIVES AND LEMON ZEST

Ingredients

2 thin tuna steaks, uncooked
Juice of half a lemon
4 Tbs olive oil
12 black olives
Zest of a lemon
2 Tbs chopped flat leaf
  parsley
Salt and freshly-ground black
  pepper

Toss cooked, drained pasta
with tuna mixture and serve at
once. Serve with conchiglie,
penne or farfalle.

This is a light and simple dish, full of contrasting flavors and colors. Basically a warm pasta salad, it requires a minimum of preparation, but it does need good, fresh ingredients to work well. Fresh tuna steaks are best, pan-fried in a little olive oil and lemon juice. They have to be well done, because if they are still raw inside they will not flake well in step 2. To flake the cooked tuna, use the point of a knife to tease it apart along the "grain" of the meat. You can use canned tuna, heated in a little oil and lemon juice, but it is not quite the same.

Use good, glossy black olives such as Greek kalamata, rather than the canned kind, which seldom have much flavor. Pit the olives first if the stones bother you – many garlic presses come with an olive pitter built into the handle.

1 *Sprinkle tuna with a little lemon juice and cook in half the oil over medium heat until well done.*

2 *Turn off heat. Flake cooked tuna and add olives, lemon zest and parsley.*

3 *Season with salt and pepper and add remaining oil and extra lemon juice to taste.*

SHRIMP AND ASPARAGUS

Ingredients

8 oz (200 g) asparagus
  spears, trimmed
1 clove garlic, crushed
4 Tbs olive oil
10 oz (250 g) large shrimp
  (prawns)
Freshly-ground black pepper

Add cooked, drained pasta
to shrimps and asparagus
and drizzle over the
remaining olive oil. Toss
thoroughly and serve at once.
Serve with tagliatelle, linguine
or spaghetti.

This simple recipe is made special by its ingredients. Pink shrimp, green asparagus tips and cream-colored noodles contribute contrasting flavors and colors. Striped tiger shrimp work particularly well, though any variety can be used, as long as they are large enough not to get lost among the asparagus.

The asparagus can be steamed over the water in which the pasta is cooking, but should not be steamed for too long. It does not need to be completely tender in step 1, as it will be cooked further in the frying pan.

As an alternative to this recipe, skip the garlic and olive oil, and dress the ingredients in a simple lemon butter. Gently fry the steamed asparagus in 3 oz (75 g) of unsalted butter, add the shrimp and cook them in the butter also. Whisk the juice of half a lemon into the pan until amalgamated. Season and toss with the cooked pasta.

1 *Steam trimmed asparagus for about 2 minutes over a pan of boiling salted water. Drain and set aside.*

2 *Fry garlic in 2 Tbs olive oil over low to medium heat until softened.*

3 *Add steamed asparagus and cook until tender, moving it about to prevent burning*

4 *Add shrimp to the pan, season with pepper and cook until they turn pink.*

CRAB AND ARUGULA

Ingredients
1 oz (25 g) butter
6 oz (150 g) dressed crab
  meat
1 dried chili, crumbled
4 fl oz (100 ml) cream
8 oz (200 g) arugula (rocket)
  roughly chopped
Salt and freshly-ground black
  pepper

Toss cooked, drained pasta
with sauce. Dress with
remaining arugula and serve
at once. Serve with penne,
farfalle, tagliatelle or
fettuccine.

In this sauce the richness of the cream and the crab meat are offset by the spiciness of the chili and the smoky taste of arugula. This recipe will make a rich first course or a filling main course and works best with chunky pasta shapes such as penne or bow-shaped farfalle, or long, broad ones like fettuccine or tagliatelle.

Dressed crab may be expensive, but when combined with the pasta, cream and arugula it goes a long way and is a perfect five-minute ingredient, since it needs no complicated preparation. Just scoop the brown and white meat out of the half shell and mix it together with a fork before adding it to the pan. Be careful not to use too high a heat or keep the crab meat over it for too long, because it can quickly become dry. The aim is just to warm the crabmeat through, rather than to cook it, since the dressed crab will already have been cooked.

1 Melt butter over low heat, add crab meat and crumbled chili and stir gently for 2 minutes.

2 Add cream and continue to stir over low heat until amalgamated and warmed through.

3 Mix most of arugula leaves into sauce. Season to taste.

SMOKED SALMON AND CREAM

Ingredients
8 oz (200 g) smoked salmon,
  thinly sliced
8 fl oz (200 ml) cream
Freshly-ground black pepper
Dill, for decoration

Toss cooked, drained pasta
with sauce and serve at once.
Serve with tagliatelle or
fettuccine.

This simple, elegant sauce will make a light main
course or an attractive first course. The strong and
distinctive flavor of salmon marries well with cream
and the combination of amber and white ingredients
makes this a delicate and attractive dish.

You will need smoked salmon that has been
pre-cut into thin leaves. Use kitchen scissors or a
sharp knife to cut these into strips.

It is important not to boil or burn the cream
when making the sauce. Use a low to medium heat
and stir regularly. The aim is just to warm the
ingredients through – there is no need to actually
cook the smoked salmon.

A few sprigs of dill added to the sauce at step 3,
and some more tossed in with the pasta at the end,
complement the salmon very well and add further
color.

1 *Cut the slices of smoked
salmon into thin strips.*

2 *Heat the cream in a small
pan over a low heat.*

3 *Add salmon strips.
Continue to heat until salmon
is warmed through. Season
with a little black pepper.*

SCALLOPS WITH CHILIES AND PARSLEY

Ingredients
1 clove garlic, crushed
4 Tbs olive oil
16 small fresh scallops (fewer if large)
1 dried chili, crumbled
6 fl oz (150 ml) dry white wine (optional)
3 Tbs chopped flat leaf parsley
Salt and freshly-ground black pepper

Toss cooked, drained pasta with sauce, garnish with parsley and serve at once. Serve with spaghetti, spaghettini or linguine.

Scallops with chili is a traditional combination, found in seaside restaurants up and down Italy. This sauce is an ideal five-minute standard – quick, spicy, and colorful. It will make an excellent first course or a light main course. Long pasta shapes like spaghetti, spaghettini or linguine are the best accompaniments. The thin, broth-like sauce of oil, wine, herbs and chili coats the strands. Make sure the scallops are well distributed among the pasta.

If you are using large scallops then cut them sideways into two or three coin-shaped rounds before frying them. Detach the orange-colored corals and add these, whole, to the pan after the white meat – they are very tender and do not need to be cooked for as long. You can make this sauce without wine, but it is not quite the same. The wine offsets the oil and complements the seafood.

1 *Fry the garlic in the oil over low to medium heat until soft.*

2 *Add scallops and crumbled chili and fry gently until scallops are almost cooked.*

3 *Pour in wine, if using, and sprinkle with two thirds of parsley. Simmer until wine has reduced slightly. Season to taste.*

SHRIMP WITH TOMATOES AND GARLIC

Ingredients
1 clove garlic, crushed
3 Tbs olive oil
14 oz (350 g) can crushed
   (pulped) tomatoes
3 Tbs chopped flat leaf
   parsley
1 dried chili, crumbled
   (optional)
8 oz (200 g) large shrimp
   (prawns), pre-cooked
6 fl oz (150 ml) dry white
   wine (optional)
Salt and freshly-ground black
   pepper

Toss cooked, drained pasta
with sauce and garnish with
parsley. Serve at once with
spaghettini, spaghetti or
linguine.

This basic sauce of tomatoes and garlic can be combined with most kinds of seafood. Shrimp have been used here, but mussels, clams, squid or a combination of these, will work well.

The sauce should have a smooth and thick consistency and so it is best to use crushed tomatoes rather than canned chopped ones, since these contain a lot of liquid and will take longer to reduce. The wine and chili in this sauce are optional – vary the amounts or omit according to taste.

Canned anchovies can also be used to make a five-minute seafood sauce. Stir six anchovy fillets into 4 fl oz (100 ml) of olive oil over a medium heat. After a few minutes, the anchovies will dissolve into the oil, to form a rich, fishy paste. Add chopped parsley and some capers, and stir cooked penne or fusilli into the anchovy sauce.

1 *Gently fry the garlic in the oil over a medium heat until soft.*

2 *Add tomatoes, two thirds of parsley, and chili if using, and simmer until mixture has reduced by about a third.*

3 *Add shrimp and wine, if using, and cook a further 2 minutes until shrimp are warmed through.*

3
MEAT SAUCES

QUICKFIRE CARBONARA

Ingredients
6 oz (150 g) thick-sliced
  pancetta or bacon, cut into
  thin strips
3 Tbs olive oil
6 fl oz (150 g) dry white
  wine (optional)
3 egg yolks and 1 whole
  egg
4 oz (100 g) freshly-grated
  parmesan
Salt and freshly-ground black
  pepper
Parsley, for decoration

Toss cooked, drained pasta in
egg and cheese. Stir in
pancetta mixture and serve
immediately with freshly-
grated parmesan. Serve with
spaghetti or spaghettini.

Carbonara is one of the classic pasta dishes, and there are almost as many versions of the recipe as there are cooks. It is often made with a cream base, but for this lighter version olive oil is used.

The heat from the cooked pasta is all it takes to thicken the beaten eggs and olive oil into a smooth sauce. The dry white wine is a foil to the egg yolks. If not using wine, skip step 2.

Pancetta is a kind of dry-cured Italian bacon. It is available smoked or unsmoked. Use whichever you prefer. If you cannot find it, then lean bacon will work just as well. Buy the bacon or pancetta thickly sliced so that when you cut it into strips they are quite chunky and will crisp well.

There are lots of ways to vary this five-minute carbonara. Add some cream to the egg and cheese mixture to make it richer; lighten it by using two whole eggs instead of egg yolks; or pep it up by crumbling a dried chili into the beaten eggs.

1 *Fry pancetta or bacon strips in a little oil until golden brown.*

2 *Add wine, if using, and let bubble and reduce slightly. Keep mixture warm on lowest setting.*

3 *Beat egg yolks, whole egg, the remainder of the oil and cheese together in a small bowl. Season to taste.*

BACON AND PAN-FRIED SCALLIONS

Ingredients

6 thick rashers lean unsmoked
  bacon cut into thin strips
4 Tbs olive oil
6 large scallions (spring
  onions), ends trimmed
Freshly-ground black pepper
Parmesan shavings, for
  decoration

Toss cooked, drained pasta
with bacon and scallions and
pour over remaining olive oil.
Serve with tagliatelle,
spaghetti or fettuccine.

Pan-fried scallions have a milder, sweeter taste
than when raw and combine well with crisp strips of
bacon and a little parmesan. This is a very
straightforward recipe which will make an informal
main course, served with fettuccine or spaghetti.

The scallions can be cooked whole and then cut
into segments, or sliced into rings and scattered into
the pasta when cooked. The bacon can be replaced
with pancetta, or strips of prosciutto either
uncooked, or crisped in a little hot oil until golden.

Try combining other pan-fried or grilled vegetables
with bacon and parmesan. Baby asparagus tips are
particularly good, brushed with olive oil and grilled
until they just begin to char; so are red onions, sliced
into rings and cooked until soft, sweet and slightly
browned. As a vegetarian alternative, combine them
with shredded arugula (rocket) leaves and parmesan
instead of bacon.

1 Fry bacon in a small
amount of the oil until crisp
and golden brown. Remove
pan from heat and keep
warm.

2 In a large pan, cook
scallions in 1 Tbs oil over
medium to high heat until
wilted and slightly browned.

3 Cut each scallion in 3
pieces and add them to the
bacon. Season with plenty of
black pepper.

PANCETTA AND CHILIES

Ingredients

2 Tbs olive oil

6 scallions (spring onions), white root ends and green shoots chopped finely and kept separate

6 oz (150 g) pancetta or lean bacon, sliced and cut into strips

2 dried chilies

14 oz (350 g) can chopped tomatoes

Salt and freshly-ground black pepper

Add cooked, drained pasta to sauce and toss well. Sprinkle over green scallion shoots and serve immediately with freshly-grated parmesan. Serve with penne or fusilli.

Arrabiata – tomato and chili sauce – is one of the standards of Italian pasta cookery and has many variations. Including pancetta or bacon makes the sauce more substantial while the chopped scallions give flavor and color. When you chop the scallions, keep the white root end and the green shoots separate. The shoots should be added at the last moment, so that they retain their bright green color.

Dried chilies are a perfect five-minute ingredient. They keep indefinitely and can be crumbled into the sauce, cutting down on preparation time. The two chilies used in this recipe will produce a noticeably hot sauce. Add the chili a little at a time until you reach a level you are comfortable with.

To make a simple arrabiata sauce, cook a finely chopped onion and a crushed garlic clove in a little olive oil until softened. Add chopped or crushed (pulped) tomatoes and dried chili; simmer until reduced and then toss with cooked pasta.

1 *Heat oil in small pan. Add white scallion ends and cook over medium heat until soft.*

2 *Add pancetta or bacon strips and cook until golden.*

3 *Crumble chilies into pan, add tomatoes and cook over a medium heat until reduced by one third. Season to taste.*

CHICKEN LIVERS WITH SAGE

Ingredients
2oz (50 g) prosciutto, cut into
   strips
4 fresh sage leaves
2 oz (50 g) butter
8 oz (200 g) chicken livers,
   cut into slices and dusted
   with flour
4 fl oz (100 ml) marsala
   (optional)
2 Tbs heavy cream (optional)
Salt and freshly-ground black
   pepper

Toss cooked, drained pasta
with sauce and serve at once.
Serve with pappardelle or
lasagnette.

Chicken livers are a great five-minute ingredient.
They are inexpensive, cook quickly, and can be
stored frozen then thawed before use. Cut away any
white, fatty strands, slice the livers thinly and, if you
want, give them a dusting of flour. Because chicken
livers cook so fast it is easy to overcook them: when
pricked with a sharp knife they should be crisp on
the outside but still pink and juicy within.

Marsala is a dark, sweet Italian wine which
combines well with the richness of the chicken
livers. It is available in Italian food shops and many
supermarkets.

To make a lighter chicken liver sauce, crush a
clove of garlic and fry it gently in olive oil until
softened. Add the sliced chicken livers and cook
them until tender (you can throw in a few shreds of
prosciutto if you have it). Stir in half a glass of dry
white wine and a squeeze of tomato puree. Stir well,
let the liquid reduce a little, season and serve.

1 *Cook prosciutto and sage
leaves in butter over medium
heat until prosciutto is golden.*

2 *Add chicken livers and
cook until crisp on the outside
but still pink and soft in center.*

3 *Add marsala, if using, and
let simmer and reduce. Over
very low heat quickly stir in
cream. Season to taste.*

PROSCIUTTO AND PEAS

Ingredients

6 oz (150 g) prosciutto, thinly
  sliced
3 Tbs olive oil
6 oz (150 g) frozen garden
  peas, thawed
Freshly-ground black pepper

Toss cooked, drained pasta
with prosciutto and peas and
serve with freshly-grated
parmesan. Serve with
spaghetti, tagliatelle or
fettuccine.

Salty amber prosciutto, sweet garden peas, a little
olive oil and a twist of black pepper make one of the
simplest and most attractive five-minute pasta dishes.

The key to this straightforward dish is the quality
of the ingredients. If you can get it, use prosciutto –
air-dried ham from Parma in Italy. It may be
expensive, but nothing has quite the same taste and
coloring. If prosciutto is not available, substitute
another dry-cured ham, thinly sliced. Bacon is too
coarse and meaty. The saltiness of the prosciutto
means you are unlikely to need to add salt.

A more traditional ham and pea sauce can be
made by adding 6 fl oz (150 ml) cream to the pan
after step 3 and cooking over a medium heat until
the liquid has reduced and thickened slightly. Season
and toss the cooked pasta in the sauce. This richer
recipe is often served with green and white fettuccine
as *paglia e fieno con prosciutto e piselli* ("straw and hay
with ham and peas").

1 *Using kitchen scissors, snip
prosciutto slices widthways
into strips.*

2 *Heat oil in small pan over
low to medium heat. Add
prosciutto and cook for about
1 minute.*

3 *Add peas and cook for 2
minutes, stirring occasionally.
Season to taste.*

PORK SAUSAGE AND ROSEMARY

Ingredients

1 small onion, chopped
  finely
1 clove garlic, peeled and
  crushed
3 Tbs olive oil
A sprig of rosemary, leaves
  stripped and chopped
½ lb (200 g) good-quality
  pork sausages or coarse
  pork sausage meat
7 oz (175 g) can chopped
  tomatoes
6 fl oz (150 ml) dry white
  wine (optional)
Salt and freshly-ground
  black pepper

Toss cooked, drained pasta
with sauce and serve at once
with freshly-grated parmesan.
Serve with penne, rigatoni,
macaroni or amori.

Pork and rosemary is a traditional combination
which, with onion, garlic and tomatoes, makes a
filling main course. With some crusty bread this is
a perfect dish for a cold winter's evening.

Use the best-quality pork sausages you can find –
cheaper varieties tend to contain a lot of "filler" –
breadcrumbs and worse. Spiral Italian sausage is
ideal; the premium brands of sausage stocked by
many supermarkets are also good. Whichever variety
you use, squeeze the meat out of the skin and break
it up roughly with a fork before cooking it.

A pinch of dried rosemary can be substituted if
you do not have the fresh herb. Unlike basil or
parsley, rosemary retains its flavor well when dried,
in fact it gets stronger, so take care not to overdo it.
If you are using sausage which is already heavily
spiced, then you may want to leave out the rosemary
altogether.

1 *Cook onion and garlic in
the oil over medium heat until
softened. Add rosemary.*

2 *Squeeze meat out of
sausage skins and break up
roughly. Add to pan and fry
until lightly browned.*

3 *Add chopped tomatoes
and wine, if using. Simmer
gently to reduce and thicken.
Season to taste.*

4
UNUSUAL
SAUCES

CREAM AND LEMON

Ingredients
2 oz (50 g) butter
Juice of one lemon
Grated zest of one lemon
8 fl oz (200 ml) cream
Salt

Toss cooked, drained pasta
with sauce and serve at once
with freshly-grated parmesan.
Serve with fettuccine or
tagliatelle.

Lemon and pasta may seem an unlikely combination
but it is one that works very well. This sauce is zesty
and refreshing, and will make an unconventional
first course. A modern Italian classic, it is also
extremely simple. A cream-based sauce of this kind
is best served with egg noodles, such as tagliatelle or
fettuccine.

Nowadays, lemons are often coated with a thin
layer of protective wax. Since you will need to use
the lemon's outer skin, use an unwaxed lemon or
wash the lemon well before grating the zest. You can
buy a zester, a tool specially designed to cut thin
strips of citrus peel, quite cheaply. If you do not have
one, then use the finest setting on a standard cheese
grater. Grate the yellow surface peel but avoid the
white pith below, which has a soapy taste. It's worth
noting that it is much easier to remove the zest
before you squeeze the lemon.

1 *Place butter in a small pan
and melt over low to medium
heat.*

2 *Add the lemon juice and
zest and stir to amalgamate.*

3 *Add cream and salt. Stir
over low to medium heat until
cream has thickened and
reduced by about a third.*

Fresh Figs

Ingredients
2 oz (50 g) unsalted butter
6 fresh, ripe figs, peeled and
    cut into small segments
6 fl oz (150 ml) cream
Salt and freshly-ground black
    pepper

Toss cooked, drained pasta
with sauce, garnish with fig
segments and serve at once
with freshly-grated parmesan.
Serve with fettuccine,
tagliatelle or farfalle.

This delicate and pretty sauce works best as a first
course, rather than as a main course. Like most
creamy sauces, it suits ribbon pasta, such as
fettuccine or tagliatelle, but will also work well with
bow-shaped farfalle.

It is important that the figs are ripe and red, to
give the dish its elegant pink color, but they must
not be overripe, otherwise they will disintegrate
completely in the pan. Take care not to overcook
them in step 2, since they will continue to cook
when the cream is added.

A small glass of vodka or better still, grappa, a
fiery Italian grape spirit, makes an excellent addition
to this dish. Add 2 Tbs (50 ml) to the pan at step 2,
let it simmer and reduce, and then add the cream.
Use a little less cream than in the basic recipe, in
view of the extra liquid. The fieriness of the spirit is
a good foil to the sweetness of the figs.

1 *Heat the butter in a small
pan on a low heat until it
begins to bubble.*

2 *Add figs, reserving a few
segments. Stir gently over low
heat for about 2 minutes until
figs begin to soften.*

3 *Pour in cream and simmer
until reduced and slightly
thickened. Season to taste.*

WALNUT AND CREAM

Ingredients

6 oz (150 g) fresh shelled
   walnut pieces
2 oz (50 g) butter
2 oz (50 g) freshly-grated
   parmesan cheese
6 fl oz (150 ml) heavy cream
2 Tbs good-quality olive oil
Salt

Toss cooked, drained pasta
with sauce and serve at once
with freshly-grated parmesan.
Serve with lasagnette,
pappardelle, fettuccine or
fusilli.

Walnuts, olive oil, cream and parmesan cheese make
a rich and pesto-like sauce, which works well as a
first course. Broad ribbon shapes, such as fettuccine
or pappardelle, or the spiral-shaped fusilli are good
accompaniments.

There are many versions of this traditional recipe.
Try substituting ricotta for cream in step 2 to
produce a grainier pesto. Raw garlic is often added,
though it can sometimes tend to overwhelm the
other ingredients. One of the best ways of
introducing a subtle undertone is to add a crushed
garlic clove which has first been softened and
mellowed by frying. If you prefer a more strongly-
flavored sauce, replace the parmesan cheese with
grated pecorino. Use a fresh packet of walnut halves
as walnuts quickly become rancid and bitter. You can
also use a mixture of walnuts and pine nuts.

1 *Place the walnuts and
butter in a food processor
and process until reduced to
a nutty paste.*

2 *Add the grated parmesan
and cream to the bowl and
process until amalgamated.*

3 *With food processor
running, slowly add oil and
process until smooth. Add
1 Tbs hot water. Season with
a little salt.*

Orange and Mint

Ingredients

2 oz (50 g) butter
Grated zest of one orange
4 large mint leaves, chopped
    roughly
Juice of one orange
Salt and freshly-ground black
    pepper

Toss cooked, drained pasta
with sauce and serve at once
with freshly-grated parmesan.
Serve with fettuccine,
tagliatelle or pappardelle.

A version of this sauce is made in Florence, using cream and grappa. In this simplified five-minute recipe the flavors of the orange and mint come through more clearly and need only a little parmesan to offset them.

This is a delicate sauce which will make a refreshing first course or a light main course. Citrus and mint may seem an unlikely basis for a pasta sauce, but the result tastes and looks wonderful. It is best served with flat noodle shapes like tagliatelle, fettuccine or pappardelle so that the orange zest and mint fleck the strands of pasta. A little cream can be added at the end of step 3, to make a richer sauce.

If you do not have a zester, grate the orange peel using the finest setting of a cheese grater and taking care to grate only the surface of the peel and not the bitter white pith underneath it. Grate the orange before you squeeze it.

1 *Melt butter in a small pan over a gentle heat.*

2 *Stir in the orange zest and mint and cook for a minute or two, keeping the heat low.*

3 *Add orange juice and simmer to let mixture reduce and thicken a little. Season to taste.*

HOT MELON AND PROSCIUTTO

Ingredients
2 oz (50 g) butter
Flesh of a large charentais or
    cantaloupe melon,
    deseeded and cut into
    cubes
6 oz (150 g) thinly-sliced
    prosciutto, torn into small
    shreds
Freshly-ground black pepper

Toss cooked, drained pasta
with the melon and prosciutto
and serve with freshly-grated
parmesan. Serve with
linguine, fettuccine or
tagliatelle.

Melon and prosciutto is a well-established
combination, often served in Italy as a first course.
The saltiness of the prosciutto is perfectly
complemented by the sweetness of fresh melon. The
partnership also works when the ingredients are
warm. Heated in a little butter, the cubed melon
juices mingle with the prosciutto to form a sweet/salt
sauce which is excellent when served in small
quantities as an unconventional first course with thin
egg noodles such as linguine.

The melon must be fresh and juicy, but not
overripe. Fragrant, orange-fleshed varieties such as
cantaloupe are particularly good. You can also use a
combination of orange cantaloupe and green galia
melon, for added contrast of taste and color. It is
essential not to overcook the melon or it will
disintegrate into a mush. The cubes need to be quite
big, so that when they soften a little and release juice
they retain some body.

1 *Melt the butter in a large pan over a low heat.*

2 *Add cubed melon and stir gently over low heat for about 2 minutes, until melon begins to soften.*

3 *Add prosciutto and warm through over low heat for about a minute. Season with a little black pepper.*

WILD MUSHROOMS

Ingredients
4 oz (100 g) butter, diced
2 oz (50 g) dried porcini, or
  morels, pre-soaked (reserve
  liquid)
16 oz (400 g) fresh oyster,
  shiitake or chestnut
  mushrooms, or a mixture of
  these, sliced
4 fl oz (100 ml) liquid used
  for soaking dried mushrooms
Salt and freshly-ground black
  pepper

Toss cooked, drained pasta
with sauce and serve at once
with freshly-grated parmesan.
Serve with farfalle, fettuccine,
tagliatelle or spaghetti.

Porcini (ceps) and morels are exotic varieties of wild mushroom highly valued for their intense, meaty flavor. Fresh ones are very expensive and hard to find, but many delicatessens sell dried porcini or morels. (The dried porcini are usually thinly sliced, while the black cone-like morels are dried whole.) A small quantity of either of these will transform fresh mushrooms by imparting a wonderfully rich flavor. Dried porcini and fresh brown chestnut or shiitake mushrooms work particularly well, but any combination of fresh mushrooms will benefit from the addition of a few of these exotic fungi. Try adding a little cream in step 3 for a richer sauce.

Dried mushrooms need to be reconstituted by soaking them in warm water for about half an hour (a breach of the five-minute rule, but well worth it). Drain the soaked mushrooms and reserve some of the soaking liquid (strain it first to remove any grit) to add to the recipe like a mushroom stock.

1 *Melt the butter in a large pan over a low heat.*

2 *Add the porcini or morels and cook gently in the butter for a minute or two.*

3 *Add fresh mushrooms and reserved liquid. Cook until mushrooms are tender and liquid has reduced and thickened slightly. Season.*

5
VEGETABLE AND
HERB SAUCES

BASIL, OLIVES AND SUNDRIED TOMATO

Ingredients

4 oz (100 g) sundried
  tomatoes
4 cloves garlic, peeled and
  bruised
12 black olives
1 dried chili, crumbled
4 Tbs extra virgin olive oil
8 large basil leaves, torn into
  pieces
3 Tbs flat leaf parsley,
  chopped finely

Toss cooked, drained pasta with sauce after removing crushed garlic. Garnish with herbs and serve with freshly-grated parmesan. Serve with spaghetti, spaghettini or linguine.

The simplest recipes are often the best. This combination of basil, olives and sundried tomatoes is colorful and full of flavor – perfect for a summer lunch or a light supper. Serve it with some crusty bread to mop up the olive oil. None of the ingredients (except the pasta) need to be cooked.

The garlic cloves should be bruised rather than crushed – raw crushed garlic would be overwhelming. Peel the cloves and squash them beneath the flat of a knife until they break open. Remove the crushed cloves before serving – a few minutes in the bowl with the other ingredients is enough for the oil to absorb the garlic flavor.

The best way to chop the sundried tomatoes is with a pair of kitchen scissors. Always tear basil leaves rather than chopping them – tearing brings out their flavor and stops them from blackening.

1   *If tomatoes have been stored in oil, drain and pat dry with kitchen towel. Chop them roughly.*

2   *Place chopped tomatoes in a large bowl with garlic, olives and chili. Mix well.*

3   *Stir in oil, basil and parsley, reserving a few herbs for garnish.*

BLACK OLIVES AND TOMATO

Ingredients

2 Tbs olive oil

1 garlic clove, crushed

3 Tbs flat leaf parsley, finely chopped

4 basil leaves, torn into large pieces

14 oz can chopped tomatoes

10 olives, pitted and coarsely chopped

Salt and freshly-ground black pepper

Toss cooked, drained pasta with sauce and serve at once with freshly-grated parmesan. Serve with penne, spaghetti or fusilli.

This tasty sauce is excellent on its own, but it can also be used as a jumping-off point for other speedy recipes. It can be served as a first course or a light main course with spaghetti or pasta shapes.

Parsley and basil have been used here, but you can vary the herbs by substituting thyme or oregano. The olives need to be good, tasty ones. Since most canned pitted olives are quite bland, it may be better to buy good-quality whole ones and stone them yourself using an olive pitter. Some garlic presses come with one built into the handle.

For a quick, spicy tomato sauce, skip the basil and olives and crumble half a dried chili into the tomatoes. You could also add some pancetta cut into thin strips, or some capers (washed and drained to remove the salt or vinegar in which they are bottled).

As an alternative to canned chopped tomatoes, use crushed (pulped) tomatoes. These have a smoother, consistency and will reduce more quickly

1   *Heat oil in pan and fry crushed garlic over low to medium heat until softened and translucent.*

2   *Add parsley, basil and tomatoes. Cook over medium heat until mixture has thickened and reduced by a third.*

3   *Add the olives and warm through. Season to taste.*

HERBS AND BREADCRUMBS

Ingredients
3 cloves garlic, sliced into
thin slivers
6 Tbs good-quality olive oil
6 Tbs (150 g) flat leaf
parsley, finely chopped
5 Tbs dry breadcrumbs
8 basil leaves, torn into small
pieces
Salt and freshly-ground black
pepper

Pour hot oil and herb sauce
over cooked, drained pasta.
Add breadcrumbs, basil and
seasoning and toss
thoroughly. Serve at once with
freshly-grated parmesan.
Serve with spaghetti or
spaghettini.

This sauce is an Italian standard. Tasty and
economical, it is best served with spaghetti or
spaghettini. The hot oil takes on the aroma of the
herbs and garlic, while the sautéed breadcrumbs
cling to the strands of pasta and add crunch. You can
vary the herbs according to what is available –
substitute fresh oregano, thyme, marjoram or a
mixture if you prefer. The herbs should be fresh, not
dried, and you will need plenty of them. If in doubt
over the quantities, always use more, not less.

Slice the garlic sideways into thin rounds, like
almond slivers, rather than into small dice. Take care
not to burn the garlic when cooking – if burnt it will
become bitter. For a gentler garlic flavor, peel just
one clove, crush it under the blade of a knife and
rub it round the inside of the pan, in place of step 1.

1 Fry garlic in 4 Tbs oil over
low to medium heat until
softened and translucent.

2 Turn heat down to low and
add parsley. Cook until lightly
colored. Set aside and keep
warm.

3 Heat remaining oil in
separate pan over medium
to high heat and fry
breadcrumbs until golden.

ARUGULA PESTO

Ingredients
12 oz (300 g) arugula
  (rocket) leaves
4 oz (100 g) pine nuts
Salt
4 Tbs extra virgin olive oil
4 oz (100 g) freshly-grated
  parmesan
1 oz (25 g) butter
Salt and freshly-ground black
  pepper

Toss cooked, drained pasta
with sauce and serve at once
with freshly-grated parmesan.
Serve with fusilli, penne or
fettuccine.

One of the most famous pasta dressings, pesto is
usually made from basil leaves, which are combined
with garlic, cheese, pine nuts and olive oil to make a
rich paste. It takes its name from the mortar and
pestle in which the ingredients were originally
crushed. This recipe is a modern variation, made
with arugula leaves – their smoky taste is an ideal
basis for a sauce. The pesto will keep in the fridge
for several days if covered with olive oil and stored
in a sealed jar to prevent the chopped arugula leaves
from blackening. (The olive oil may congeal in the
fridge, but will be fine when brought back to room
temperature.)

To make a traditional basil pesto, substitute 12 oz
(300 g) of fresh basil leaves for the arugula and add
half a crushed garlic clove to the mixture in step 1.
Thereafter, the recipe is exactly the same.

1 *In food processor chop
arugula, pine nuts, a pinch of
salt and oil until fine and
almost creamy.*

2 *Add parmesan and
process until it has been
amalgamated.*

3 *Add butter and 1 or 2 Tbs
hot water and process until
smooth. Season to taste.*

ZUCCHINI WITH CREAM AND SAFFRON

Ingredients

12 oz (300 g) zucchini
(courgettes), cut into
matchsticks
2 oz (50 g) butter
8 fl oz (200 ml) cream
¼ tsp saffron powder
Salt and freshly-ground black
pepper

Toss cooked, drained pasta
with sauce and serve at once
with freshly-grated parmesan.
Serve with fettuccine or
tagliatelle.

Saffron is made from the stigmas of the crocus flower. It imparts a vivid yellow color and a subtle flavor to food. Pound for pound, saffron is one of the most expensive spices because it is so labor-intensive to harvest, but as here, it is generally used in extremely small quantities. Delicatessens and supermarkets sell little sachets of saffron powder or strands. If you are using saffron strands, soften them in a teaspoon of warm water before adding them to the cream.

To make the zucchini sticks, top and tail the zucchini then halve them lengthways. Slice each half into thin strips, and cut these into two-inch (5 cm) lengths. There is no need to peel the zucchini. The contrast between their green skin and the delicate yellow cream is an important part of the dish.

1 *Melt butter in a pan over low to medium heat.*

2 *Add zucchini and cook over medium heat until golden but not soft.*

3 *Reduce heat to low. Add cream and saffron. Cook, stirring frequently, until cream has reduced by almost half. Season to taste.*

RADICCHIO AND ONION

Ingredients

1 medium-sized mild onion, roughly chopped

2 Tbs olive oil

6 fl oz (150 ml) dry white wine (optional)

12 oz (300 g) radicchio, roughly chopped

Salt and freshly-ground black pepper

6 oz (150 g) arugula (rocket), roughly chopped, for decoration

Toss cooked, drained pasta in the onion and radicchio mixture, garnish with arugula and serve at once with freshly-grated parmesan. Serve with fettuccine or tagliatelle.

Radicchio is a bitter red salad leaf which combines well with the sweetness of fried onions. This is a light and unusual sauce, best served as a first course, with fettuccine or tagliatelle, to which the oil and wilted vegetables will cling. Chopped arugula leaves or a little chopped flat leaf parsley sprinkled over the finished dish add contrasting color and flavor.

The wine offsets the oil and is an important ingredient in this recipe though you do not need to use a lot. If you do not want to use wine, cook the onion in butter (add a little oil to prevent the butter from burning) and when the radicchio has wilted in step 3, add 4 fl oz (100 ml) cream to the pan, stirring until it is thoroughly mixed in and warmed through. Season and serve at once.

As a variation on the basic recipe, try using a mixture of radicchio and Belgian endive (chicory) in step 3, which will give a slightly different flavour.

1 *Fry onion in oil in small pan over a medium heat until soft and translucent.*

2 *Add the wine and let it simmer and reduce.*

3 *Reduce heat to low. Add radicchio and let it wilt and soften. Season to taste.*

INDEX